OLYMPIC SPORTS

SWIMMING AND DIVING

by Clive Gifford

amicus

Published by Amicus
P.O. Box 1329
Mankato, MN 56002

Printed in the United States of America, at Corporate Graphics,
in North Mankato, Minnesota.

Library of Congress Cataloging-in-Publication Data
Gifford, Clive.
  Swimming and diving / by Clive Gifford.
      p. cm. — (Olympic sports)
  Includes index.
    ISBN 978-1-60753-192-0 (library binding)
  1. Swimming—Juvenile literature. 2. Diving—Juvenile literature.
      3. Olympics—Juvenile literature. I. Title.
  GV837.6.G55 2012
  797.2—dc22

                                                    2010046934

Created by Appleseed Editions, Ltd.
Designed by Helen James
Edited by Mary-Jane Wilkins
Picture research by Su Alexander

Picture credits
page 4 Getty Images; 5 iPhotos/Shutterstock; 6 Sports Illustrated/Getty Images;
7 Getty Images; 8 AFP/Getty Images; 9 Herbert Kratky/Shutterstock; 10 Sports
Illustrated/Getty Images; 11t Schmid Christophe/Shutterstock, b Gert Johannes
Jacobus Vrey/Shutterstock; 12 Sports Illustrated/Getty Images; 13 AFP/Getty
Images; 14 Getty Images; 15 AFP/Getty Images; 16 Sportgraphic/Shutterstock;
17 Getty Images; 18 & 19 AFP/Getty Images; 20 Getty Images; 21 AFP/Getty Images;
22 Getty Images; 23t Marcello Farina/Shutterstock, b AFP/Getty Images; 24 AFP/
Getty Images; 25 Pete Saloutos/Shutterstock; 26 Goldenangel/Shutterstock;
27t AFP/Getty Images, b Goldenangel/Shutterstock: 28 Getty Images;
29 l AFP/Getty Images, r Getty Images
Front cover: Sportgraphic/Shutterstock

DAD0051
3-2011

9 8 7 6 5 4 3 2 1

Contents

Going for Gold

The Olympics are the biggest single sporting event in the world. Once every four years, the world's elite athletes battle it out for the coveted Olympic gold, silver, and bronze medals. The action takes place over 17 unforgettable days, watched by millions on TV, the Internet, or live at the stadium.

FEATS AND RECORDS

At the 2008 Olympics, the design of the pool in Beijing meant that the water was deeper than usual. The extra depth may have contributed to the amazing 25 swimming world records that were set during the 2008 Olympics.

Tony Azevedo of the U.S. tries to pass the ball as Hungary's Tibor Benedek defends during the men's water polo final at the 2008 Olympics. Players are fast-moving and athletic, and water polo draws loyal fans to every Olympics.

SWIMMING START

In 1896, 18-year-old Alfréd Hajós from Hungary became swimming's first Olympic gold medalist when he won the 100 meter **freestyle** race at the Athens games—the first modern Olympics. Swimming has been a part of every Olympics since, joined by water polo in 1900, diving in 1904, and synchronized swimming in 1984. All these sports are grouped together as aquatics.

Superstar

Johnny Weissmuller won five Olympic gold medals for swimming at the 1924 and 1928 Olympics before he played the role of Tarzan in 12 movies. He is not as well-known for being part of the U.S. water polo team, which won a bronze medal at the 1924 Olympics.

Olympic OoPs

The outdoor pool complex at the Athens 2004 Olympics had no roof. This led to complaints from competitors and spectators about the lack of shade from the blazing sun.

NEW AND OLD

Some aquatics events have made just one appearance at the Olympics. These include an underwater swimming race, the longest underwater dive and the 4,000 meter freestyle. Women's water polo and synchronized diving were introduced in 2000, and a 10 kilometer **open water** race came along in 2008.

AQUATICS CENTERS

Most Olympic swimming, diving, and water polo events take place in an Olympic aquatics center. Olympic pools are 50 meters (164 ft.) long, twice as long as a regular pool. Events are measured in meters since the pool is measured in meters. The London 2012 aquatic center, with its distinctive wave-shaped roof, will hold as many as 17,500 people.

The National Aquatic Center at Beijing was the location for the swimming and diving events for the 2008 Olympics. The center was nicknamed the Water Cube and held 17,000 spectators.

Starting and Finishing

The competitors in the 100 meter butterfly semi-final at the 2008 Olympics react to the starter's gun. They power off the blocks into a shallow, fast dive.

A good start and a fast, accurate finish help champion swimmers turn a good race into a great one and succeed at winning an Olympic medal.

EIGHT LANES

An Olympic pool is divided into eight racing **lanes** that are usually 2.5 meters (8.2 ft.) wide. There are empty lanes along both sides of the pool. The swimmers' lanes are separated by rows of plastic discs or floats, which help reduce the waves from the swimmers' movements. At each end, there is a turn judge. This is an official who checks that every swimmer makes a turn within

the rules and, in longer races, shows swimmers how many lengths or laps they still have to swim.

A RACING START

All races (except for backstroke events) start when swimmers step onto a starting platform or **block** in front of their pool lanes. They adopt the ready position and wait for the starter's orders. As soon as they hear the starter's signal

—usually a pistol shot—they dive off their blocks and into the water. They are allowed to glide up to 15 meters (49.2 ft.) underwater before surfacing.

FALSE STARTS

A swimmer who leaves the block early makes a false start. New competitive swimming rules mean that this **disqualifies** them from the race. Officials drop a rope across the pool 15 meters (49.2 ft.) from the start to let the other swimmers know if this happens.

FAST FINISHES

Top swimmers try to speed to the pool wall as they near the finish. They try to time their strokes perfectly so they touch the wall with outstretched fingertips. Pressure-sensitive touch pads on the wall are connected to electronic timing systems that display the swimmers' times. These are measured to hundredths of a second, which is usually enough to separate the positions in a race.

Olympic OoPs

At the 2001 World Swimming Championships, Giaan Rooney completed the 4 x 200m relay race for her Australian team in first place. Her teammates leapt into the water to celebrate before the other teams had finished. This was against the rules, and the Australian team was disqualified.

FEATS AND RECORDS

In 1984, Carrie Steinseifer and Nancy Hogshead, both from the U.S., swam the first recorded official dead **heat** at an Olympics. They swam the 100m freestyle in 55.92 seconds, and both won a gold medal.

Katie Hoff of the United States looks up at the scoreboard to see if she has qualified for the next round of the 800m freestyle competition at the 2008 games.

Freestyle and Butterfly

Swimmers compete using one of four swimming strokes: front crawl, breaststroke, backstroke, and butterfly. Many competitions, including the Olympics, include freestyle events that allow swimmers to choose any stroke. Front crawl is the fastest stroke, so all the swimmers use this.

Yuriy Prilukov of Russia (top) swims head to head with Canada's Ryan Cochrane in the 1500m freestyle at the 2008 Olympics. The swimmers' arms sweep through the air alternately, then plunge into the water in front of them.

FREESTYLE RACES

The length of freestyle races ranges from long distance 800 meter and 1500 meter events (see pages 16–17) to the fastest event of all, a dramatic short sprint over one length of the pool. Competitors use the powerful front crawl stroke, keeping their bodies flat in the water and turning their head to one side to breathe.

SOMERSAULT TURNS

Freestyle swimmers practice and perfect their turns at the ends of the pool so they lose as little time as possible between lengths. They use a slick, underwater somersault, known as a **tumble turn**, to start a new length making a powerful push off the pool wall with their feet.

BUTTERFLY

The most spectacular swimming stroke is the butterfly, and this is also the newest stroke. It was developed during the 1930s, and swimmers first used it at the 1956 Olympics in the men's 200 meter and the women's 100 meter events. Men and women now compete over both distances in very close races. In the 100 meter butterfly final at the 2008 Olympics, Michael Phelps beat Serbia's Milorad Čavić by just one hundredth of a second.

BUTTERFLY TECHNIQUE

In the butterfly stroke, a swimmer swings the arms forward together, skims low over the water, and plunges into the water hands first. The legs and feet move together in a movement called the dolphin kick. Butterfly swimmers must finish their race by touching the pool wall with both hands.

Austria's Nina Dittrich competes in the 200 meter butterfly. The stroke is extremely tiring, so top swimmers have to be amazingly fit.

Breaststroke and Backstroke

Swimmers first swam backstroke at the 1900 Olympics, and breaststroke was introduced eight years later. Competitors race over 100 meters and 200 meters at the Olympics, as well as take part in **medley** races (see pages 14–15).

U.S. swimmer Rebecca Soni competes in the 200 meter breaststroke. As she completes the gliding phase of breaststroke, she will sweep her arms outward.

BREASTSTROKE

Breaststroke is a very precise stroke. Swimmers make perfectly symmetrical strokes as they glide with their arms out in front. They then pull back their arms in a wide sweep, before pulling them in again to start another glide. At the same time, the swimmer's legs kick out together in a movement like a frog's. When they make a turn and finish a race, breaststroke swimmers have to touch the pool wall with both hands. Touching the wall with both hands together saves time.

NOT SO SLOW

Breaststroke is the slowest of the four strokes, but top swimmers still complete a full length of the pool in about 30 seconds. At the 2008 Olympics, Kosuke Kitajima of Japan smashed the world record for the 100 meter breaststroke with a time of 58.91 seconds. Kitajima went on to win both the 100 meter and 200 meter gold medals just as he had done in 2004 in Athens.

BACKSTROKE

Backstroke is sometimes known as the back crawl because the arm and leg movements are similar to those in front crawl, but performed facing upward. The swimmer's legs kick like a whip from the hips as the arms reach up and behind the swimmer and pull them through the water.

BACKSTROKE STARTS AND TURNS

Olympic swimmers compete in 100 meter and 200 meter backstroke events. They begin facing the pool wall, coiled like a spring and gripping handles on the starting platforms. On the starter's signal, they launch themselves back and under the water. The head must surface within 15 meters (49.2 ft.) of the start or they are disqualified. Swimmers are also allowed to swim up to 15 meters underwater after each turn.

A backstroke swimmer's arm passes straight past his ear before entering the water directly in front of his head.

Backstroke swimmers grip the handles on their starting blocks. As the race starts, they push off strongly, fling their arms back, and arch their backs so their hands enter the water first.

Superstar

Aaron Peirsol is one of the fastest ever backstroke swimmers. He won six Olympic gold and two silver medals at the 2004 and 2008 Olympics and was unbeatable in the 100 meter backstroke between 2002 and 2009.

Relays

Swimming relay races are dramatic, action-packed events for teams of four swimmers. Each swims the same distance as their teammates, and at the changeover, the next swimmer dives into the pool.

Lacey Nymeyer dives into the water just after her U.S. freestyle relay teammate completes her swim and touches the pool wall. The U.S. team won a silver medal at the 2008 games.

RELAY RULES

At the Olympics, both men and women swim in relay races, swimming 100 or 200 meters per leg. All relays are freestyle events, so swimmers use the front crawl. A swimmer must touch the pool wall to complete their leg of the relay. Only then can their teammate leave their starting block and dive into the water.

TEAMS AND SELECTION

Relay teams usually have more than four swimmers. This means that strong teams can rest one or more of their best swimmers in some rounds, bringing in another member to replace them. In the 2008 women's 4 x 200 meter relay, the victorious Australian women's team included eight swimmers, while the Chinese team, which came in second, had only five swimmers. Any swimmer who takes part in the heats but not the final wins a medal if their team wins one.

HUGE RIVALRY

The rivalry between the U.S., China, and Australia women's swimming teams and between the men's U.S., Australian, and French swimming teams has produced some astonishing races. At the 2008 Olympics, the U.S. team seemed beaten in the 4 x 100 meter final, before Jason Lezak swam the fastest 100 meter relay leg in history, allowing the Americans to beat France by just 0.08 seconds.

BREAKING SEVEN MINUTES

The first 4 x 200 meter record was set by the British team at the 1908 Olympics, with a time of 10 minutes 55.6 seconds. At the 2008 Olympics, the U.S. team, led by Michael Phelps, became the first to swim the race in less than seven minutes. This had once been thought impossible, until the U.S. covered 800 meters in 6 minutes 58.56 seconds.

The Netherlands 4 x 100m women's relay team laughs as the scoreboard confirms they have won gold at the 2008 Olympics. Their time of 3:33.76 was a new Olympic record.

FEATS AND RECORDS

In the men's 4 x 100 meter relay at the 2008 Olympics, there was a series of astonishing performances. The African, Asian, European, and world records were all broken in the heats, and all eight teams in the final swam faster than the winning team from South Africa in 2004.

Superstar

Gertrude Ederle won a gold medal in the 4 x 100 meter freestyle relay team at the 1924 Olympics. Two years later, she became the first woman to swim the English Channel.

Medleys

Medleys are events in which swimmers compete in all four of the major swimming strokes over set distances in a race. There are team and individual medley events.

From left to right, Lisbeth Trickett, Jessicah Schipper, Leisel Jones, and Emily Seebohm of Australia celebrate winning gold in the women's 4 x 100m medley relay. The quartet set a new world record time of 3 minutes 52.69 seconds.

INDIVIDUAL MEDLEY

Most swimmers specialize in one, or sometimes two strokes, but a swimmer competing in the individual medley (IM) has to work hard on all the strokes in order to perform powerfully and accurately in a race. At the Olympics, swimmers compete in individual medleys over 200 and 400 meters. Each swimmer begins the race by diving into the pool, and then swims one or two lengths of butterfly, before swimming equal distances of backstroke, breaststroke, and finally, freestyle.

DOUBLE DUEL

At the 2008 Olympics, Zimbabwe's Kirsty Coventry and Stephanie Rice of Australia competed in both the 200 and the 400 meter individual medley. Rice won the races, but both swimmers swam the 400 meter medley in under 4 minutes 30 seconds for the first time, and both broke the world record in the 200 meter race.

TEAM MEDLEYS

Four swimmers take part in team medleys, with each swimmer performing one stroke in one leg of the relay race. The one Olympic competition is the 4 x 100 meter for both men and women, which was first held in 1960.

STROKE ORDER

The team medley begins with the first swimmer in the water as the race starts with backstroke.

This leg is followed by one each of breaststroke, butterfly, and finally freestyle. Just as in other relay races, one swimmer has to complete a leg and touch the wall before the next team member can leave the block. At the 2008 Olympics, the top 16 men's and 16 women's teams competed in two heats. The eight fastest teams took part in the final.

FEATS AND RECORDS

The U.S. has an astonishing record in the men's 4 x 100 meter medley. They have won every gold medal except at the 1980 Olympics, which the U.S. team **boycotted** and Australia won.

A member of the German women's 4 x100m relay team dives in at the 2004 Olympics. She had to wait until her teammate had completed her swim and touched the pool wall before diving.

Long Distance Swimming

Races that are longer than 400 meters are long distance events in competitive swimming. The international swimming organization **FINA** holds world championships every two years. Here, both men and women race over 800 and 1,500 meters. At the Olympics, they each take part in one long distance event—the 800 meter for women and the 1,500 meter for men.

Grant Hackett powers through the water. Top long distance freestylers perfect their front crawl style so they minimize the energy they use with each powerful stroke.

THE 800 METER FREESTYLE

In the past, the longest events for women were the 400 meter freestyle and individual medley competitions. That changed in 1968, when American Debbie Meyer won the first women's 800 meter freestyle with a time of 9 minutes 24.0 seconds.

LONG DISTANCE CHAMPIONS

Swimmers are completing the 800 meter faster and faster. Many 800 meter Olympic

Superstar

Grant Hackett set a world record of 14 minutes 34.56 seconds in the 1,500 meter freestyle at the 2001 World Championships. He also won the 1,500 meter freestyle at the 2004 Olympics, only to discover afterward that one of his lungs had partly collapsed, reducing his breathing ability by around a quarter.

the mile (1,609 m) race. They swim using the powerful front crawl stroke, and the top swimmers complete each length of the pool in less than 30 seconds—an astonishing speed to keep up over 30 lengths. In the 1,500 meter final in 2008, long distance swimming legend and world record holder Grant Hackett was beaten by Oussama Mellouli from Tunisia.

champions have been American, including Brooke Bennett and Janet Evans, but recent winners include Japan's Ai Shibata in 2004 and Britain's Rebecca Adlington in 2008.

HEATS AND THE FINAL

In both 800 and 1,500 meter competitions, competitors have to swim heats. At the 2008 Olympics, there were five heats in the men's 1,500 meter race. All the swimmers in the heats are timed, and the fastest eight enter the final.

THE 1,500 METER FREESTYLE

Swimmers have competed in the toughest long distance pool race, the 1,500 meter, in every Olympics since 1908 when it replaced

Superstar

In 2008, Rebecca Adlington became the first British swimmer to win more than one gold medal at one Olympics since Henry Taylor in 1908. Taylor won the 4 x 200 meter relay, the 400 meter freestyle and the 1,500 meter freestyle, in 22 minutes 48.4 seconds.

Rebecca Adlington punches the air as she not only wins the Olympic 800m freestyle final, but breaks the world record by 2.12 seconds, a huge margin.

17

Open Water Swimming

Open water swimming in lakes, rivers, and the sea has become a popular aquatic sport. FINA has run open water swimming world championships since 2000. At the 2008 Olympics, men and women competed in 10 kilometer (6.2 mile) open water races for the first time.

The mass start of the women's 10 kilometer open water race at the 2008 Olympics. The competitors dive into open water at the Shunyi Rowing and Canoeing Park in Beijing.

MASS START

Swimmers qualify for the Olympic event by performing well in qualifying races held months beforehand. At the 2008 Olympics, 25 swimmers competed in each race. Racing begins with a mass start. There is much buffeting and accidental contact between swimmers in the early stages of the race.

ENERGY SAPPING

The 10 kilometer race takes top swimmers a little under two hours to complete. All use the front crawl. This race is an endurance test as swimmers compete over a distance equivalent to 200 lengths of an Olympic pool, or 6.2 miles. They may meet strong currents in the water, as well as wind, which makes the surface choppy with waves. Swimmers often swim right behind an opponent to conserve energy. This technique is called **drafting**.

Natalie du Toit during training at the 2008 Olympics. Du Toit was the first leg amputee to qualify for an Olympic swimming event.

FEEDING STATIONS

The 10 kilometer event is a swimming marathon, and swimmers have feeding stations along the way. These are floating **pontoons** in the water where the swimmers' coaches dangle sports drinks on poles above the water. A swimmer can grab a drink, swallow it, and continue swimming all in two or three strokes. Many swimmers carry edible gel packs inside their swimming suit as well.

CLOSE FINISHES

At the finish of a race, swimmers have to cross a line and touch one of several touch pads. Above the touch pads are cameras that record photo finishes. Although the swimmers compete over a long distance, there are often close finishes. At Beijing, British swimmers Keri-Anne Payne and David Davies were both overtaken near the finish line. Both won silver and both finished just 1.5 seconds behind the winners, who were Maarten van der Weijden of the Netherlands and Russian Larisa Ilchenko.

Superstar

Natalie du Toit lost her left leg below the knee in a car accident. Yet she finished fourth at the 2008 Open Water World Championships, so she qualified for the Olympic 10 kilometer race. She finished sixteenth, and weeks later, won five gold medals at the **Paralympics**. She carried the South African flag at the opening ceremonies of both the 2008 Olympics and Paralympics.

Diving

Divers compete by springing from a flexible springboard or a solid high platform above a deep pool. While in the air, they perform a series of acrobatic moves before plunging cleanly into the water.

Tom Daley leaps high above the board as he begins a dive during the 2008 Olympics. Daley was just 14 years old when he took part in these games.

OLYMPIC ORIGINS

Diving was one of the first Olympic sports in which women could take part. They first competed in diving in 1912, eight years after the first men's event. At the Olympics, men and women compete in two different events, the springboard, which stands 3 meters (9.8 ft.) above the water, and the platform, which is 10 meters (32.8 ft.) high.

CLEAN ENTRY

A dive lasts less than two seconds, yet during that time, top divers perform extraordinary acrobatics. They turn multiple somersaults and twist with such precision that they are perfectly vertical by the time they enter the water, hands first, often at speeds up to 31 mph (50 km/h). A great dive can be ruined by a splashy entry, so competitors try to punch as small a hole as possible in the water.

FEATS AND RECORDS

The 2½ somersaults with 2½ twists pike dive is one of the hardest of all. At the 2008 Olympics, Australian Matthew Mitcham stunned spectators and rivals by performing an almost perfect dive, scoring 112.10—the highest single dive score ever at the Olympics—to win the men's 10 meter gold medal.

DEGREES OF DIFFICULTY

There are dozens of different dives. Some start with the diver facing backward or performing a handstand. Each dive has a degree of difficulty (**DD**) number depending on how hard it is to how good an entry they make into the water. This score is multiplied by the dive's degree of difficulty, then multiplied by 0.6 to give a final total. Divers perform many dives in the preliminary competition at an Olympics, then the top 18 divers enter the semi-finals. The 12 highest-scoring divers in the semi-finals compete in the final. At any time, even a small error in a dive could mean the end of their medal chances.

perform. On a 3 meter springboard, a single forward somersault dive in a tucked position has a low DD of 1.5. At the other end of the scale, a difficult dive with four and a half backward somersaults and a tuck has a DD of 4.3.

JUDGING AND FORMAT

Judges score each dive on how well its different parts are performed, the diver's position, and

China's Guo Jingjing is tucked tightly during a dive at the 2009 World Championships. Jingjing won the competition. She appeared at four Olympic games from 1996 to 2008.

Synchronized Diving

There was an exciting new series of diving events at the 2000 Olympics in Sydney. Synchronized, or synchro, diving takes place on both the 3 meter springboard and the 10 meter platform for men and women.

ROUNDS OF DIVES

Pairs of divers perform different rounds of dives. The competition specifies some dives, and others are chosen by each pair of divers. The divers need to perform all the movements of their dive in perfect harmony and enter the water at exactly the same time to earn a good score. This takes years of intensive training.

PICKING PARTNERS

Diving pairs must be a similar build and height so they can perform the dives at the same speed and with similar ease. The 2008 gold medal winners of the 10 meter synchronized diving, Wang Xin and Chen Ruolin, were almost exactly the same weight.

SYNCHRO SCORING

Seven judges usually judge an individual dive, but there are nine judges for synchronized diving.

Divers Lin Yue and Huo Liang leave the platform 10 meters (32.8 ft.) above the pool at Beijing's National Aquatic Center. The Chinese pair won gold at the 2008 Olympics.

Two judges for each diver assess individual performance, while a panel of five officials judges how well the two divers are synchronized as they dive.

Legendary Chinese diver Guo Jingjing and her partner, Wu Minxia, compete at the 2009 World Championships. The pair won the gold medal.

Wang Xin (right) and Chen Ruolin show great symmetry as they perform tucked somersaults at the 2008 Olympics competition.

Superstar

Chen Ruolin was only 13 when she won the 10 meter synchro dive at the Asian Games in 2006. She was just 15 when she won the Olympic competition with her partner Wang Xin in 2008. Chen was also FINA World Champion in 2007 and 2009 in the 10 meter synchro.

FEATS AND RECORDS

Thomas Bimis was 32nd and Nikolaos Siranidis 36th in the individual 3 meter springboard event at the 2000 Olympics. Teamed together in the 3 meter synchro four years later, the pair won gold, Greece's first ever diving medal.

Synchronized Swimming

Synchronized swimming is a combination of swimming, water gymnastics, and dance. Competitors need to be strong, flexible, and graceful, and also have excellent timing to perform their routines.

The Japanese synchronized swimming team performs a spectacular move, positioned vertically underwater. At the 2008 games, Japan finished joint fifth with the U.S.

AT THE GAMES

Synchronized swimming was a demonstration sport at many Olympics before it became a medal sport at the 1984 games. Three events have been held, all for women only: a team event for eight swimmers, duets for two, and a solo event. There were solo events at the 1984, 1988, and 1992 games in which individual swimmers performed routines.

TECHNICAL AND FREE

Duets and teams perform two routines. The technical routine has moves and positions that must be performed in a set order. The free routine is set to music and lasts about four minutes for the team event and three minutes, 30 seconds for the duets. Swimmers choose their own music and moves for the free routine.

MAKING MOVES

Swimmers cannot use the bottom of the 10 foot (3 m) deep pool for support. Instead, they use a powerful water treading technique called the **eggbeater** to rise up out of the water, and perform spectacular moves by themselves, or to lift teammates. They also perform elements underwater, where special speakers allow them to hear the music so they can stay in time.

MARKS AND MEDALS

A panel of ten judges marks each routine. Five mark the technical accuracy of the moves, while the other five judge the artistic merit of the performance. This includes assessing how well a duet or team interpret the music they perform to. At first, swimmers from the U.S., Canada, and Japan were most successful, but teams from Spain, France, and Russia have been medal winners in recent years. Russia has won the most Olympic gold medals in the sport.

Olympic OoPs

At the 1992 Olympic synchronized solo competition, a judge accidentally typed in a score of 8.7 instead of 9.7 for Canadian Sylvie Fréchette, so she lost the gold medal to Kristen Babb-Sprague. Sixteen months later, Fréchette was also awarded a gold medal.

FEATS AND RECORDS

Anastasia Yermakova and Anastasia Davydova have won at recent Olympics. They won both the 2004 and 2008 duet events and were part of the Russian team, which won the team competition in both 2004 and 2008.

A synchronized swimming team practices a move at the surface. Moves are rehearsed intensely over many months so that all members of a team can perform perfectly.

Water Polo

A water polo goaltender stretches, but cannot stop the ball from flying into the goal. A water polo goal is 9.8 ft. (3 m) wide and is anchored in place in the pool.

Sportsmen first played water polo at the 1900 Olympics. Exactly 100 years later, women's water polo became a medal event at the Sydney Olympics. This fast, action-packed ball sport is played in a large pool. Teams try to score goals by throwing the ball into a 9.8 foot (3 meter) wide goal that sits on top of the water.

GAME TIME

A water polo team includes 13 players, with seven (six outfield players plus a goaltender) in the pool at any one time. Players are regularly substituted during the game, which is divided into four periods of eight minutes. The game clock is stopped whenever the ball is not in play, so a period usually lasts around 11 or 12 minutes. The players begin each period with a sprint swim for the ball from their own goal line.

FEATS AND RECORDS

Dezsö Gyarmati has more Olympic water polo medals than any other athlete. He won silver with the Hungarian team in 1948, three gold medals (1952, 1956, and 1964), and a bronze in 1960.

China's Sun Huizi prepares for a powerful throw during a game against Russia at the 2008 Olympics. China won the game 13–11.

ATTACK!

The team who wins the ball attacks. They have 30 seconds to score a goal, otherwise the ball passes to the other team. A player can use any part of the body to move the ball across the top of the water or throw it with one hand.

They cannot dunk the ball below the surface or punch it with a fist. Players try to push themselves up as high out of the water as possible to free an arm and make a throw.

Water polo players have to be extremely fit and strong. They swim the front crawl to reach the ball or defend against an opponent and need to tread water well. Top players may swim 3 miles (5 km) during a game. They are not allowed to touch the bottom or the sides of the pool.

Defenders around the goalmouth try to cut off offenders and block shots. During a game, the ball can travel at 56 mph (90 km/h).

Olympic OoPs

In a 1972 Olympic water polo game between Hungary and Italy, eight Hungarian players were suspended for fouls in 38 seconds! Hungary still won the game 8–7 and went on to take a silver medal.

Gold Medal Greats

Swimmers, divers, and water polo players have to train long and hard to make it to the Olympics. Only a handful reach the peak of their sport and win Olympic medals. Here are four of the greatest ever aquatic performers.

MICHAEL PHELPS

Michael Phelps finished fifth in the 200 meter butterfly final at his first Olympics in 2000. He made up for any disappointment four years later, winning an incredible six gold medals and two bronze medals, all at the age of 19. At the 2008 games, he achieved feats that many thought were impossible. He swam 17 races in nine days to win an astonishing eight Olympic gold medals, beating Mark Spitz's record of seven gold medals at the 1972 games.

FEATS AND RECORDS

In addition to his Olympic medal haul, Michael Phelps has won an incredible 23 gold medals at world championships, including five in the 2009 competition.

Michael Phelps wins the 2008 Olympics 200m individual medley final. He set a new world record time of 1 minute 54.23 seconds.

REBECCA ADLINGTON

Rebecca Adlington beat American favorite Katie Hoff to win the 400 meter freestyle at the 2008 Olympics, the first gold medal won by a British woman swimmer since 1960. Her performance in the 800 meter freestyle was even more amazing. She smashed swimming's longest-standing world record (set by Janet Evans in 1989), recording a time of eight minutes 14.0 seconds to win by over six seconds. Adlington won three golds at the 2010 British trials and is training hard for the 2012 Olympics.

GUO JINGJING

Known as the princess of diving in China, Guo Jingjing started diving when she was six years old. She first appeared at the Olympics in 1996 and in 2000 won two silver medals. She is a specialist at the three meter springboard, both as an individual diver and as a synchro pair with partner Wu Minxia. Guo won two gold medals at both the 2004 and 2008 Olympics. She continues to excel at springboard events, winning her ninth and tenth world championship gold medals in 2009.

Manuel Estiarte Duocastella powers out of the water to launch a throw at the 1984 Olympics.

MANUEL ESTIARTE DUOCASTELLA

Manuel Estiarte was one of the finest water polo players of all time. He was born in 1961 and first appeared at an Olympics in 1980. He played more than 580 games for the Spanish national team. He appeared at six Olympics, winning a silver medal in 1992 and a gold in 1996, beating the U.S., Hungary, and Croatia along the way. In four of his six Olympics, he was the tournament's highest scorer, and he scored a record 127 goals in Olympic competitions.

Guo Jingjing springs off the board as she practices a dive. The Chinese diver won four Asian Games gold medals to go with her Olympic medals.

Glossary

blocks   the raised platforms at one end of the pool from which swimmers in freestyle, breaststroke, and butterfly races begin

boycott   to refuse to attend a competition as a protest about something

DD   short for degree of difficulty, it is a number that measures how tough a particular dive is to perform

disqualifies   taking a swimmer out of a race and not counting their performance because they have broken a rule

drafting   in open water swimming, to swim closely behind another swimmer in order to save energy

eggbeater   a way of treading water strongly to stay above the water's surface in water polo and synchronized swimming

FINA   short for *Fédération Internationale de Natation*, this is the organization that runs world swimming, diving, and other aquatic sports

freestyle   races or events that allow competitors to swim any stroke; this is usually the front crawl as it is the fastest swimming stroke.

heat   an early race in an event that qualifies the fastest finishers to compete in the semi-final or final of an event

lane   a narrow corridor in a swimming pool down which a swimmer swims in a race

medley   an event in which one swimmer or team swims each part of the race using one of the four major strokes: backstroke, breaststroke, butterfly, and freestyle

open water   long distance swimming races, usually held over 5 kilometers (3 miles) or longer, in a river, lake, or sea

Paralympics   the major sports competition for elite athletes with a disability that takes place in the weeks after an Olympic games

pike   a position in diving where the diver's body is bent at the hips and the legs are straight

pontoon   a boat or floating platform from which coaches hand open water swimmers food or drink

tumble turn   an underwater turn at an end of the pool that lets the swimmer push off for the next length with their feet

Books

Michael Phelps by Mike Kennedy (Gareth Stevens Pub., 2010)

The Olympics: Unforgettable Moments of the Games by Stephanie Peters (Little Brown & Co., 2008)

The Olympics: Scandals by Moira Butterfield (Sea-to-Sea Publications, 2012)

Swimming, Diving, and Other Water Sports by Jason Page (Crabtree Pub., 2008)

Swimming Science by Helene Boudreau (Crabtree Pub. Co., 2009)

Web Sites

www.olympic.org/sports/
This web page lists all the sports in the Olympics. Click on a sport for information on how it is played, Olympic champions, and much more.

www.fina.org/H2O/
The official web site of the organization that runs world swimming has news and features on swimming, diving, and water polo.

www.usadiving.org
USA Diving oversees training and preparing the U.S. Olympic diving teams, and serves as a source of information on all aspects of the sport.

www.waterpolo.ca/rules.aspx
A clear explanation of the basic rules of water polo.

www.10kswim.com/starts.html
A web site about the ten kilometer (6.2 mile) open water swim, with photos of techniques and tactics.

Index